Let's Find Ads on the Internet

by Mari Schuh

first step nonfiction

Lerner Publications ◆ Minneapolis

LERNER

e

SOURCE™

Expand learning beyond the printed book. Download free, complementary educational resources for this book from our website, www.lerneresource.com.

Main body text set in ITC Avant Garde Gothic Std Medium 21/25.
Typeface provided by International Typeface Corp.

Lerner Publications Company
A division of Lerner Publishing Group, Inc.
241 First Avenue North
Minneapolis, MN 55401 USA

For reading levels and more information, look up this title at www.lernerbooks.com.

Library of Congress Cataloging-in-Publication Data

Schuh, Mari C., 1975–
    Let's find ads on the Internet / by Mari Schuh.
        pages cm. — (First step nonfiction : learn about advertising)
    Includes index.
    ISBN 978-1-4677-9464-0 (lb : alk. paper) — ISBN 978-1-4677-9661-3 (pb : alk. paper) — ISBN 978-1-4677-9662-0 (eb pdf)
    1. Internet advertising—Juvenile literature. I. Title.
    HF6146.I58S38 2015
    659.14'4—dc23   2015016194

Manufactured in the United States of America
1 – CG – 12/31/15

Table of Contents

What Is an Ad?

Ads try to sell **products**.

BAKED WITH REAL CHEESE ————

An ad can be a picture.

Cereal Commercial

An ad can be a video.

Sometimes an ad is mostly words.

Companies and Ads

Companies use ads to help sell their products.

Banana Boat® Kids UltraMist™
and Baby Pump Sprays are now

tear-free.

The only tear-free
sunblock lotion sprays.

Ads give information about
the products.

An ad can show what a product looks like.

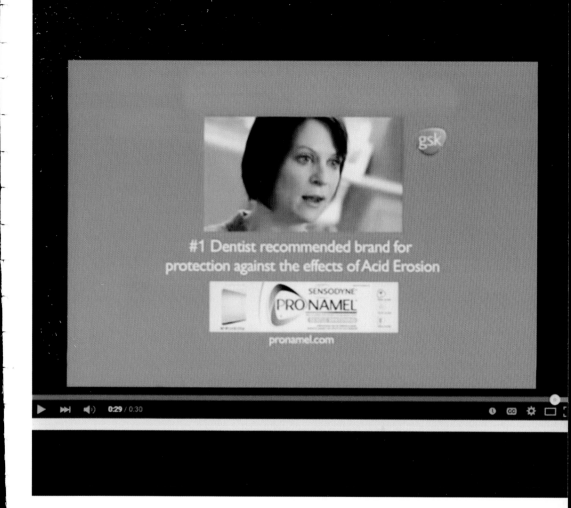

An ad can show what people think about the product.

11

Ads on the Internet

Many companies put ads on the **Internet**.

Kids use the Internet for homework and for fun.

People work and play on the Internet.

People visit **websites** on the Internet. Many websites show ads.

Ads with movement may catch your eye.

Some ads are videos.
Some ads flash or move.

15

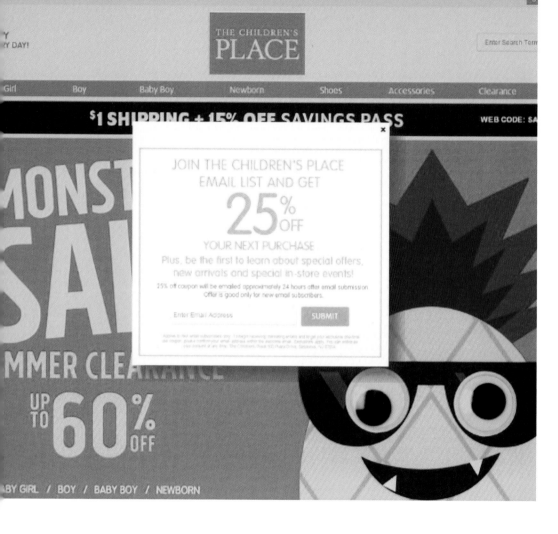

Some Internet ads pop up
on the screen.

Some ads are at the top of a website.

You can block some Internet ads. Then those ads won't show up.

Some ads tell the truth.

Some ads do not.

Some ads are a part of games or music.

Do you think this ad is telling the truth?

It's smart to ask questions about ads.

Glossary

ads – messages that try to sell products or services

companies – groups that make or sell products or services

Internet – a network that connects computers around the world

products – items that are made and sold

websites – pages on the Internet that give people information

Index